Chasing Valor

Quinton Bailey

Introduction by Lindamichelle Baron

Presentation by *BookLeaf Publishing*

Web: www.bookleafpub.com

E-mail: info@bookleafpub.com

ISBN: 9789358736137

First edition 2023

I dedicate this book to all of those (men and women) who desire to walk in valor but also desire to walk in grace.

You are not alone.

"For where your treasure is, there will your heart be also."

(Matthew 6:21 KJV)

ACKNOWLEDGEMENT

I want to humbly acknowledge God, without Him, none of this would be possible.

PREFACE

I have always been fascinated with knights and knighthood. There have been many tales of courage and chivalry that have been in lore for hundreds of years, even in time knights evolved from being cavalrymen to individuals dedicating their lives to Christian ideals. With this evolution, knights came to be accepted, for their respect for the church, protection of the poor and the weak, and loyalty to one's feudal or military superiors. A knight held steadfast to their preservation of personal honor through valor. These words here are testimonies to the battles of life that God has brought me to and through. Valor is not something that happens, it is the way of brave, purposeful living, not just when one is in danger. In God's kingdom, we are not just called for our bravery and strength, but also to be mighty.

We are called to be more...

We are called not only to chase valor but to instill it in our hearts.

TABLE OF CONTENTS

Introduction by Lindamichelle Baron

A few years ago I saw a wonderful message from a young man who indicated that he remembered me as a poet who visited his first grade class. He remembered my poetry, that I had books of poems, and that he had written a poem during or following my visit. What a blessing to be remembered decades later. But the greatest blessing of all is when he indicated that he now writes poetry, and was inspired to do so by remembering that early interaction. He then honored me with the opportunity to read his book of poetry and respond. I was prepared to appreciate his writing no matter what. I encourage all to write and share their writing as they grow. But what a pleasant surprise, when I could enjoy his book of poetry, Chasing Valor, and smile and feel the painful moments along with him.

Quinton Bailey's poetry speaks of love. The longing of love. The desire to be assured of being love. The loss of love. So many permutations of the feelings associated with love are captured in his poems.

Yes, I know, there are millions of love songs, love stories and love poems. There is a reason for that. We never get tired of love. We all need it. We have all experienced the ins and outs, ups and downs of love.

I enjoyed Quinton's take on the emotion. It was clear, direct and lovely. Thank you so much for sharing your book with me. I enjoyed reading it the first and second time. That's a great part of a short book, even with a busy schedule, there's time to read it and even reread it. I invite all to enjoy!

Dr. Lindamichelle Baron,
Associate Professor, Author, Poet Laureate, for the Town of Hempstead, New York

A Silent Knight

The young Squire (Gunbir) peeked into her
chamber like he always did every night. Even
though he was young and weak, he prayed and
watched over Princess Tenyiel, especially at
night. He heard the hushed rumors amongst the
merchants and monks about the horrors of the
night since the sun went black days ago. While
such matters did not move his spirit, Gunbir
maintained his faith in God's protection.
God has always kept a watchful eye over both of
them, but the Squire obliged to give God a hand
or a dirk every so often. Tenyiel jumped up out
of her slumber and peered into the darkness.
Trying to adjust her eyes was nearly impossible
with the candles blown out. The Princess
thought she heard a slight stirring in the room...

"Who dares?" She hissed in a voice reserved
only for those who crossed her.
Tenyiel's hand slowly reached for the 'special'
dagger that Gunbir left secretly under her
pillows.
She was ready, she was always ready.
It could have been a bat or an owl catching a
mouse, but Tenyiel knew better.
Or...
It could have been HIM.
Gunbir was indeed getting better in his nightly
movements so much that it was unsettling.
She will speak of this to him in the morn.
"You are getting better she whispered, but I can
still feel your heartbeat in the night."
She waited for a response, or even the sound of a
shuffle to affirm that the Squire was indeed
there. After what seemed like an eternity of
straining her ears to hear anything other than the
usual night sounds, she gave up and closed her
eyes.
"Hmmmmph!" She clumped her head into the
soft pillows out of frustration. "You win."
Tenyiel then heard Gunbir's voice, or did she? It
was such a soft whisper...
"G'nite, m'lady, I am never too far."
The Princess shot up, startled not knowing if
what she heard was because she longed for the

Squire so, or was it just her heart speaking to her
things that she always longed to hear?
Tenyiel laid back down with a small grin,
allowing herself to slowly drift into the land of
dreams:
That place where she spent most of her time
amongst the sunflowers with her beloved.

The Answer

What more can I say?
As I lie here awake, another day has gone.
My thoughts always lie with you.
I watched you tonight like I always have.
I watched you in terror.
There is something about you that makes me
want
To run away as fast as I can and never look back.
I always feel like there is so much more I can
give you,
But for some reason, I am afraid that I don't.
I guess when you really are in love with
someone, you always feel that way.
A part of me says that everything that you have
been through…

You deserve to have it all:
All those things that God has for you.
I close my eyes and think.
I think this time (slowly) about you, your life,
and then us.
I think of all those things…
Every day, there are going to be missed
opportunities and times
When I feel like I should have told you things
that I didn't.
The trick is not to hate myself for it…
Just accept that I am trying, and that next time I
will try harder.
Then it will get a little easier.
I am afraid to begin a lifetime together, because
I already know THE ENDING.
I think again.
All I can do is share with you all that people can
share and never waste a moment of it.
As I still lay here and look at you, I've been
asking myself,
"How, when the time came, would I ever be
strong enough to face that one ultimate fear?
Suddenly, (as if sensing my thoughts) you turn
over and whisper in my ear,
"I love you, baby."
It is then that I am reminded of the answer.

My heart-that moment

From the very first time we met, I could not take
my eyes off of you even for a second.
Ever since, I could not stop thinking of you.
From that moment on, I knew what my heart
wanted: what my heart needed was you.

When I am close to you, my heart makes me do
crazy things.
I do all of the things to make you smile.
No matter how short of a time that we spend
together, to my heart, those moments feel like
forever.
Just to be with you, and see you smile, is enough
to make me happy.

Your smile is that moment that I could NEVER
forget.
My heart takes your smile at that moment and
makes it last forever.
Indeed, I love you.

Inarticulate

The key to growth is learning to understand each other… To build up 'our language'.
We are learning a new language together.
It can be difficult if one has never spoken this language before.

One messes up, they stumble, bumble, tumble, and rumble.

Trying to understand and 'speak' this new language is hard,
Because we think we know but we don't.
Words may sound the same, feelings may be familiar,

But in the end, IT IS NEW...
Brand new, things we never experienced before.
The key is making the effort, a real honest raw
effort, to learn and never stop learning.
You have to learn that it is a necessary process
for growth.

One that cannot be jumped through or speeded
up.

It serves its time as it does,
Step by step,
Lesson by lesson.
Let GOD and the commitment to love be the
guiding force in this.

Silhouettes

In the beginning, perfection…
We waltzed together for years, without stepping
on each other's toes.
In unison, we danced.

The outline of each other…
My hands, your feet, your words, and my voice;
My thoughts, your emotions, our needs
Overlap at all the critical moments.
You laughed when I smiled.
You cried when my eyes turned red.
Now, we lie separated, by a barrier of shadows.
Reminded us that it is okay to step on each
other's toes...
after all these years.

Those hands…

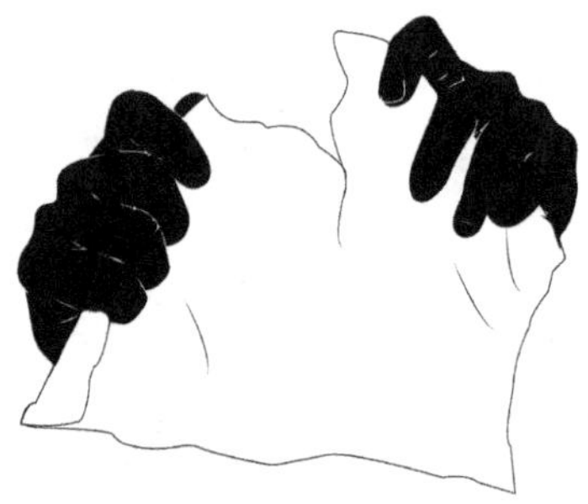

The day they touched mine, electricity flowed
        through my body.
Those soft delicate hands…
        it was so hard to let you go, because I
did not want
        to lose you.
Those soft delicate beautiful hands…
        they melt my heart, and set my soul
ablaze.
        Caressing me: they boasted of your love,
        love that showed me that I was also
beautiful.
Those soft, delicate beautiful, warm hands…
        grow harder, coarser, and colder with the
passing of time.
        Your love becomes hatred and
misunderstanding.

Your hands turn into fists. pounding my
heart and soul,
       leaving me
battered and bruised.
   I knew I loved you, but I was wrong to
hold on…
   believing and hoping that you would
change.
Those deceitful hands…
   I did not see the slow changes-
     even that moved faster than my
eyes could see.
Those misdirected and twisted hands…
   I followed them everywhere.
   They spoke to me, and left me lost
   Your hands told me of love, and of your
hate.
     They showed me that I was
beautiful
They showed me that I was ugly.
Those same hands that offered to help me up
when I was down, stay just out of my grasp.
So I reach for something that is no longer
there.
   I should have walked away,
     but I did not want to lose the
memory of those hands…
   which touched upon mine, never letting
me go.

Through the Looking Glass

It is the reflection that stares at me when I look
in the mirror, not the other way around.
So much has bothered it recently (I know).
So much that it had to stop and look at ME in
the mirror.
Unnecessary details lead to distractions.
Things it should have taken care of if only he
had the motivation to do it then, and to do it
right.

I ask the reflection:
"What exactly has taken so much space in your
life, that has forced
Or covered up your better qualities?

What in your life has taken over that smile of
yours even though it was never pretty to begin
with?"

The reflection said nothing.

And I ask again,
"What exactly is it you are looking or waiting
for?"
Weary of my questions, the reflection turned its
back on me.
I see the scars and bruises as reminders of the
rough life we both had to live.

Then the reflection spoke,
"I want to shut my eyes and when I open them
again, maybe everything will be gone, including
you.
I wish that I was asleep, so I do not have any
more of these foolish thoughts and shut off my
mind and have peace for a while."

With that statement, my reflection turned and
looked at me.
I stared back at it squarely in the face and said,
"Things will get better. You have to be strong
and have faith in us.
I am here to help you as you are here for me.

It's hard to explain, but I know that we can make
it for you and me.
Don't worry about your confidence for your wit,
and your charm have never left you.
We have to make room for the better things in
our life."
Then for the first time,
the reflection smiles (at me)
although its smile this time was never pretty to
look at.

another woman

(Note to reader: this is meant to be read fast)

Overflowing anger...
    I see the way you look and smile at her
the way you used to look and smile at me
actions speak louder, did you care dare stare for
another woman were you there for other
women-me. Always here for you all of you all
of me there for you where are you together with
the other not with me games whatever they may
be how long could I not have all of you you can
never have all of me but my overflowing anger.
Why must you lie through these unfaithful
words estranged as it may seem only pleasure I
can have as I please is only in magic moments

she will never know of your true love she can
only conceive believe perceive the stolen nights
and pleasures your treasures that only I posses
am I right this night belongs to her belongs to
me always belonging to you.

Lonely tension...
      A sick panic I feel when you are not
here not there with another-the other woman the
other women how alone without those jewels
those things she holds precious I may not be her
but I have what is hers the things she wishes for
the most what's mine what's hers where are you
now with the other woman-another woman I
love you she loves you what's right right wrong
wrong right wrong what's left nothing but me
and my lonely tension. The other woman how
do you love now then who was it me or just
another woman knowing that she is there behind
those same eyes that same smile that look at her
the way they used to look at me that other
woman-another woman could it be...me?
I hate those other women I hate me.

What Matters

I remember walking with you in the subway
underground.
All of a sudden, my wedding ring- my promise
of love to you popped off my finger and fell to
the ground.
Each bounce on the cold stone platform was
louder than a cracking shell.
I screamed as I dove to the ground in an attempt
to catch it before it went over the edge into the
tracks.

I failed.

I knew then it was over.
I knew that in spite of my best efforts this
wedding ring-
My wedding ring could not fit me.
It was too big for me.

While it was not always like that, over the years...

I changed, you changed, we changed.

Still, it was my finger that the ring fell off of.
What little did I do to ensure that it would never happen?

Nothing. I allowed that.

You then stated casually, "Let it stay there, don't get it, it's okay."
Your tone was not one of concerns for safety.
This was different.
There was a cool calm to your words, that brought me to a horrific realization-
You were done.
Done, telling me that I should be careful.
Done, telling me that I should be aware.
Done, telling me to focus, because the little things can be big things and the big things can be little.
Done, telling me how important the wedding ring is and was.

Time sometimes makes things get bigger or smaller.

I did not listen.

I did not listen, as I jumped into the train tracks totally indifferent to the dangers.

Every single fiber of my being was focused on getting the ring back on my finger where it belonged.
My soul screamed to the universe, "GET THE RING, DON'T LOSE IT, SHOW HER THIS ONE TIME HOW TRULY IMPORTANT IT IS TO ME NOW, SHOW HER THAT I DID NOT CARE ABOUT THE RISKS, THAT IT IS ALL WORTH SHOWING HER NOW THAT IT ALL MATTERED, THAT IT ALWAYS MATTERED!"

In reality, it did not matter.

"Let it stay there, don't get it. It's okay."

Those words crush me up to this day.

It was too late because I realized that as I picked up the ring and jumped back up to the platform, in the midst of everyone's screams...

THAT I WAS TOO LATE.

It no longer mattered how big or small my finger was to keep the ring on.

What mattered was that
IT WAS TOO LATE, to save the ring.
It fell into the tracks long ago.

It's all me

Some call it inspiration, some call it poetry,
others say imagination,
But I just call it a part of me.
I don't know how I write it, and don't know
exactly why.
All I know is that it is me;
It is every laugh and cry.
It takes me back to days gone by, and reminds
me of who I was.
It shows me who I am, and shows me what time
does.
It holds my hopes, my dreams, my fears, my
passions, and my pains.

It's my smile when I'm happy, and my umbrella
when it rains.
It's good at keeping secrets when I just need to
confide,
And it makes a warm shelter, for those times I
need to hide.
But it's also so much braver than I could ever be,
Because it says so much, so silent it reveals
what's inside of me.
When even I don't know, it makes me realize
what I feel.
It's my subconscious inspiration, that helps me
grasp what is real.
And I don't know how I write it;
It's what some call poetry.
Each laugh I laugh, each cry I cry,
All I know is...it is me.

Do not doubt

Do not doubt how much I love you.
Although the time together has been thin.
I am always thinking of you,
And always loving you within.

All I ever wanted is in you: love, laughter, and a
pillow for my fears.
I want to give and to be given to...
So I can feel you through our years.

I do the best that I can do,
And hope that you will understand.
Everything belongs to you: my thoughts, my
heart, and my hands.

Thank you for the things that you do.
This happiness is not in vain.
Although I am dancing to the moon,

I know obstacles still remain.

You take away those trivial things as petty, and
simple as they may be.
Your thoughts, your heart, and your hands;
all of which you have given to me.

Wilderness

I wandered in the wilderness so deep,
Where shadows danced and secrets lay in
keeping,
The path obscured, the night a shroud so wide,
But deep within, I felt a fire inside.

I yearned to find my way, to break the chains,
To leave behind the doubts, the endless pains,
Through tangled woods and darkness all around,
I sought a path, a way to higher ground.

With every step, I left the past behind,
Embracing hope, a new beginning, I would find.
The wilderness may challenge and dismay,
But it can also teach us to find our way.

So, if you're lost in the wild unknown,
Remember that your spirit can be grown.
For in the heart of darkness, you can see,
God places where you are meant to be.

Knight Time

In days of old, a Christian knight did ride,
With faith as armor, by his Savior's side.
His sword, a symbol of the Word of God,
In battles fierce, he'd never be flawed.

A beacon of light in a world so dim,
He fought for justice, casting out sin.
With a shield of faith and helmet of salvation,
He stood strong against every temptation.

His heart was pure, his purpose divine,
In God's service, he'd always shine…
Defending the weak, upholding the meek,
A Christian knight, virtuous and unique.

In a world of chaos, he brought forth peace,
His devotion to Christ would never cease.
A Christian knight, both humble and brave,
In God's love, he'd eternally engrave.

With faith as his armor, a beacon so bright,
A Christian knight, a champion of light.
In God's grace, he'd forever stand,
A symbol of faith in a troubled land.

What is a friend?

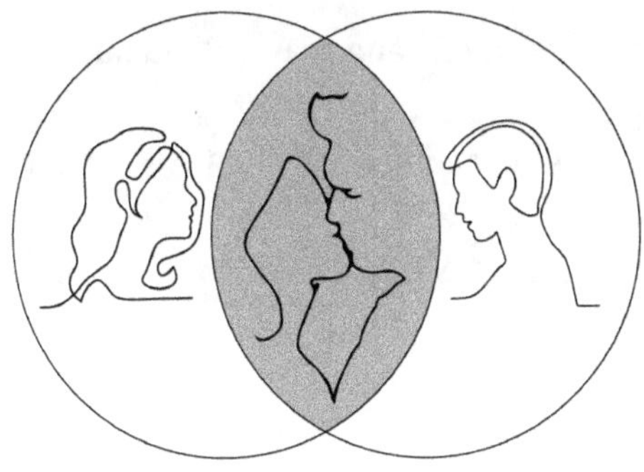

Let me tell you:
It is a person with whom you dare to be yourself.
Your soul can be bare.
They seem to ask you nothing, only to be what
you are.
They only want you to be the best version of
yourself.
You do not have to be on your guard.
They understand those contradictions in your
nature that lead others to misjudge and
misunderstand you.

With them, you breathe freely.
You can reveal your little vanities and
absurdities
And in opening up to them, they are lost in the
air of loyalty.

Best of all, you can keep still with them. It
makes no matter: they understand.

You can cry, laugh, and pray with them.

Through it all, and underneath, they see, they
know,
AND THEY LOVE YOU.

A friend?
What is a friend?
It is a person…
I repeat, with whom you dare to be yourself.

At times

When I look at you, I can hardly believe that you
are mine.
I think about how attractive, caring, sensitive,
interesting, and funny you are.
I can hardly believe that out of this whole world
of people,
I was lucky enough to find you.
I remember what it was like in the beginning
When we were just getting to know each other.
I never forget that nervous excitement I feel, or
that smile every time I see you.
I relive the tenderness of our very first kiss.
That delicate electricity still flows through my
body.
Sometimes, when I look at you, I get lost in the
memories of special times we shared.
In those daydreams of happiness, we have yet to
discover together.

That is why every time I look at you,
I realize how much I love the love we share,
And how very much I love you too.

Home

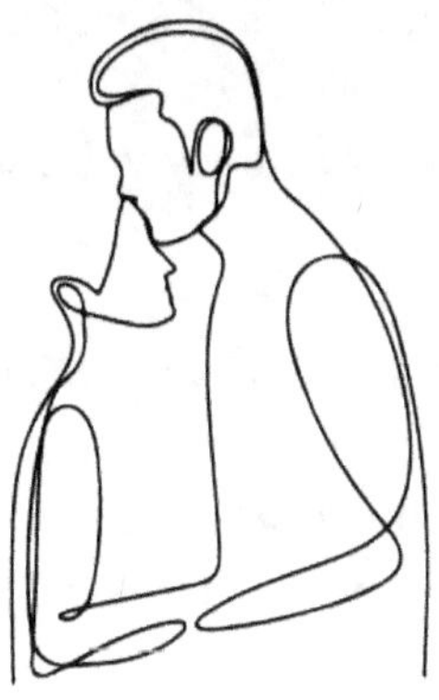

Where my voice used to be…
Remember it was you who called me your home,
Not just a mat, at your front door.
Inside is where you said you wanted to be.
The one thing that we can count on is the
passion and coincidence of you and me.

We never held back.
Holding each other tight without holding each
other at all.
Being involved without being involved at all.

I love you, it chokes me to say it.
I love you, it saddens me to feel it.

Nothing is owned up to, we merely borrow,

What we need at the moment.
Looking through the windows,
We catch only glimpses of what thought we
wanted,
And silence from where my voice was.
That's all.

Ignoring the chance of having to let go at any
given moment, the gift of each other.
We made everything we shared or had in
common THAT coincidence which kept us
together.
Just being there caring deeply, but not really
caring at all.
Everything, including that cool passion, and
those heated comments, is one part of another.
Yet, I was happy that even for the longest of
times or the briefest of moments,
I was that mat at your front door.

A Lonely Night

I will write the saddest poem ever tonight.
I can write things like…
"I miss you, and I know we will be together
again someday,
No matter how long it takes."
I wish upon not one star but all of them.
You were the first beautiful girl in the world.
I try to mark each star in the sky for every
reason I love you.
I always lose count…
I can write the saddest poem like no other
written before.
I loved her and sometimes she loved me too.

On nights like this…

I would hold her in my arms,
And kiss her for every star-
For every wish seen and unseen.
She loved me and sometimes I loved her!
How could I not love that beautiful face?
I am writing the saddest poem ever.
To think I don't have her; to see that I have lost
her.
To feel that immense night; more immense
without her.

This poem leaves my soul like a shooting star.
What does it matter, that my love could not keep
her?
There are other beautiful girls in this world.
The night is full of stars again, and she is not
with me this time.
Far away a soul, that which is not mine, sings.
Far away from me, but never having that one
chance,
That one night to be with me.
She was beautiful and she was my girl.
My soul is lost without hers.
As if to bring her nearer, my eyes SEARCH for
her.
My heart aches for her,
And she is still not with me.
It is the night that embraces me this time.
We, we who were, we are the same no longer.

My soul is lost without hers.
I never loved her much, but I truly loved her
always!
My voice pleads with the wind to touch her ears.
Nothing, but silence.

Someone else.
She will be someone else's kisses and tight
embraces.
This night is mine and mine alone.
I no longer love her truly, but perhaps I can love
her like I never did before.
I just wrote the saddest poem ever.
Love is so short, and oblivion is so long.
To think that on a night such as this, I want to
hold her tight in my arms again.
And even though this may be the last pain she
caused me,
This will be the last poem I write to her.

Between Friends

In so many ways you've touched me,
In so many ways I can name it.
You've made my entire life different,
Without you, my days are the same.
Your true friendship is so radiant,
Your understanding of me is so clear.
Whenever I am far from you,
I know in my heart you are near.
Words could never express, the emotions I keep
inside.
I thank you for all those times, that I ever
laughed or cried.
Good times you always made better,
And in bad times you always made good.
If there was anything I could not do,
I only asked once, and you would.
You know my thoughts before they are said.
You even know them before they are conceived.

You know me as I know myself.
You're the friend every person has sought.
While many spend a lifetime in futile search
Of a friend no truer than you.
Most never find what they're looking for,
But thank God, for me that's not true.
I thank God for you at all times.
I love Him and give Him my praise,
Because He has sent me an angel
To comfort me all of my days.
He has sent that angel in you, I know because I
know of no one purer.
With the three of us together as friends,
There's not a thing the Lord, you, and I can't
endure.
That bond that is between us, my friend, a
million miles never would part.
My lips do not tell you these words, not at all,
for they come from my heart.

Angel

Through fate and coincidence, a person floats by
you,
Like a feather or a dandelion on the wings of
life.
You wish and wish at the chance to get to know
them,
To dance with them,
To sing with them,
Or to even laugh with them.
You try to smile...
Then they are gone… caught in an updraft of
circumstance.
You are left feeling lost with one less person;
And fewer experiences in your life.
You look to the skies for wishes…

Wishes that even the stars cannot grant you.
I wanted to know how to dance, sing, or even
laugh with you.
        You smile...
For you remember how time flies;
The way it did when we first met.
Then you were gone… caught in an updraft of
circumstance.
I was left lost, with one less person;
And fewer experiences in my life.
You keep smiling,
While thousands of stars grin back at you.
I longed to catch that dandelion or feather,
Or to even laugh with your stars.
Still, I wish, and wish I got to know you better.

Island

A fragmented existence…
Lingering between goodnight and goodbye.
Floating in the icy wind…
You shudder under my gaze:
COLD and EMOTIONLESS.
I hold you passing all of this heat from my body
from my heart.
Just floating-NO drifting,
about and apart from each other.

A woman cries
on those shores fearing that hour of fragmented
existence
when not even that promise returns with the
waves that slap against those jagged shores of
this island.

This just does not happen.

We cry…
as we sway between that memory and tomorrow.
Our hands dangle awkwardly at our sides.
We stare-
never touching…hoping to retrieve some piece
of a tattered oath:
A promise to part as lovers, but to return as
friends.

I cry, because you don't.
A COLD AND EMOTIONLESS GAZE.

Floating in the icy wind.
I rather it be like this…
peaceful
but very lonely.
I brace myself against that chill, while you brace
yourself against me.

Knight's End

"My sweet, heroic knight," Tenyiel sighed,
"Your acts of valor have not only touched the
hearts of thousands but have also touched my
soul."
"You fought many a battle and have yet to fight
many more.
But alas, the battlefield that is my heart lays
war-torn and tired."

Tenyiel's heavy gaze and words seemed to draw
additional weight onto Gunbir even though he

knelt down in front of his queen, fully armored, head down.

"You will always be that courageous boy who dreamed of flying and slaying ALL of the dragons."

The queen reached down to the knight, but stopped herself, as she knew from the shadows they were being watched.

They were ALWAYS being watched.

"I understand your highness," Gunbir mumbled. That once thundering boom of a voice was reduced to just a whisper,
"This is love that we walk according to His commandments.
This is the commandment, that as you have heard from the beginning, you should walk in it."**

Tenyiel's guilty heart knew this scripture well.

Gunbir raised himself to leave.

It always fascinated her that Gunbir was the one knight, that you could not hear the familiar clang that carries in the air when a knight moves.

As he exited the throne room, Tenyiel felt her heart exit with him.

**(2 John 1:6)